FRIENDS

FRIENDS

We All Have Them

J. T. Windom

To order additional copies of this book, contact:
Xlibris
1-888-795-4274
www.Xlibris.com
Orders@Xlibris.com
747118

CONTENTS

Acknowledgments vii

Sean.. 1

Tommy 4

Buck 7

Tommy 10

Sean... 13

Buck 16

Tommy 22

Sean... 31

Buck 42

Tommy 45

Buck 50

Sean... 54

Tommy 58

Notes 77

Acknowledgments

To my daughters who have suffered with mental health and have showed great strive in getting the help they need to move forward and the willingness to share their story with others, thank you for allowing me to share your story in a way that will open up a dialogue to talk about mental health and to help stop the stigma surrounding it—bring education and understanding to others. Love you, girls.

To my husband who has shown great support and love through it all. You are our rock leading and holding us up, moving us forward, and constantly reminding us that God is in control, and everything is going to be all right. A man of God and truly a man after my own heart, I love you, handsome.

Thank you to my Lord and Savior Jesus Christ. Your word has given me strength, comfort, and the wisdom to understand the situation and not give up in the mist of my storm. I will keep moving forward as you have already worked it out.

Sean

I met Sean at what I like to call the Gerontology Club. Everyone in there was sixty-five years or older.

I was there with my godmother, Hazel. Earlier that day, I had picked her up from the airport. She had flown in from Alabama after burying her sister. She wanted to go for a drink to wind down and take her mind off things. She suggested going to the American Legion Post in Los Angeles, near the LAX Airport.

While sitting at the bar, a gentleman came over and bought me a drink. Although he wasn't pleasing to the eye, I appreciated the gesture. Just when I turned around to say thank you, I was distracted by a handsome face looking my way.

I wasn't sure the guy was looking at me until I leaned back from the bar and our eyes met.

He was five foot nine inches with a toned, athletic body, caramel-colored skin, a baldhead, goatee, and a gorgeous smile. He was wearing a white fitted shirt, showing off his muscles. Did I mention he had a fine, athletic body? Because if I didn't, the gentleman who bought my drink surely did notice. The gentleman saw me focused on the handsome face and not him. As I watched the gentleman walk away, I smiled and thought to myself, "At least I got to keep my drink."

Hazel and I were at the Post for several hours.

The handsome guy never came over to introduce himself or ask me to dance, but he kept looking over in my direction.

After a while, Hazel was tired and ready to go. I really wasn't ready because I was hoping the handsome guy would say something to me before we left, but he didn't approach me. As Hazel and I walked out, I felt nervous because we had to walk past him.

Once again, I thought he was going to say something to me, but he didn't. He let me walk out without saying anything—after all that looking and teasing.

When Hazel and I got to the car, I was telling her how cute the handsome guy was.

"What guy?" she asked.

I replied, "The one with the bald head and goatee."

"Winnie, they're all bald headed," she said.

And we laughed.

"No, Hazel, the one wearing a white fitted shirt, standing by the exit door with the two older gentlemen."

I asked her to go back inside to get him. And she did! When he came out to meet me, I learned his name was Sean. We talked for a few minutes, exchanged phone numbers, and our journey began.

Tommy

Tommy and I met in a unique way. After talking on the phone with Sean for several weeks, we decided to meet at the Cheesecake Factory for dinner. I love their Greek salad, chicken samosas, and the signature drink, ultimate margarita. If you haven't tried it—it's a must.

Sean and I really hit it off. Several hours passed and we were laughing and carrying on like we didn't want the night to end. When Sean went to the restroom, a very attractive guy came over to introduce himself to me. His name was Tommy.

I was excited, and nervous at the same time, because I had never done anything like that before. I was about to give the man my number while I was out on a date with someone else. I know what you're probably thinking, but I was a beautiful, single, five-foot-nine woman—what most men would call *redbone* with curves that won't quit, and my weave was always on point.

So yes, I'm a keeper and easy on the eyes, but there's more to me *than meets the eye*. I'm a very accomplished woman. For the past seventeen years, I have worked as the director of a nonprofit organization. I own several real estate properties, and I have my own business. I'm dating and looking to have fun. For the record, I do admit the way I met Tommy was a trashy move.

Tommy was nice and special in his own way. His behavior was off the chain at times. I learned early on that Tommy was the type of guy you kept behind closed doors. Can you say *dine in* only?

When he introduced himself, he said, "My name is Tommy, but they call me Tom-Tom for short." I found that quite odd as the nickname seemed longer to me.

He had caramel skin and a bald head. Yes, I guess you can tell I like bald guys. Tommy had a big heart, was very giving, and would give you the shirt off his back, if you asked him. He had two kids, a daughter and a son.

I also have two kids and they have both left the nest. The oldest daughter works and lives on her own, and the youngest daughter is in college. I couldn't wait for the day to come. My girls are six years apart, and when the youngest daughter was a senior in high school, I was counting down the days she would go off to college.

I love my girls, and I'm proud of the job I accomplished with raising them after my divorce, but I was ready for them to find their own independence so I could take my life back and have some me time.

I admit when I stepped back on the dating scene, I wasn't big on dating men with children, but after meeting Tommy, I had a change of heart. He added something different to the relationship that I had never experienced before.

One day, Tommy and I were at his house and he wanted to go to the park. Right away, I shut it down by saying, "Tom-Tom, I had a long day. Let's order in and have a movie night." He was so easygoing that whatever I wanted or said, he agreed.

Buck

B uck was a truck driver, whom I met one day when leaving Tommy's place. He was coming up the stairs when our eyes locked onto one another. He, too, was bald and good looking. He had that very attractive southern thing going on without the gold teeth. Buck loved his job, and at times, I felt he loved it too much. When talking to him about his day and he shared something exciting that'd happened, he ended his speech, saying, "My name is Buck, I drive a truck, and I love to fuck."

I would admit it scared me the first time I heard him say that. I was thinking, "I hope he doesn't expect me to fuck him every time he says that, because he says it lot."

With him being on the road a lot, it worked out perfectly for me, dating and all. But whenever he was in town, we did make time for each other.

Buck was a very aggressive person who spoke his mind. He didn't take crap from anyone, and I felt safe with him. I liked that quality in a man, someone who wasn't going to run off, leave me there to fight the battle, or turn into the comedian Kevin Hart and ask, "Why did you say something to that man to make him angry. If you get slapped, you just get slapped."

After being divorced for over five years, it was hard for me to move forward. I didn't think I would ever open myself up again to let another man get close to me. When I was going through counseling, they recommended reading the book *Boundaries, by Cloud and Townsend*. The book talked about boundaries and writing down what boundaries were important to you and use your list when dating, and if the person was crossing one or more of your boundaries, then you should cut your losses and move on. It was still early in the game, but for that moment, he wasn't crossing my boundaries, and he made my needs paramount.

My sister, Tamaika, didn't like Buck. She thought he was a bully, and she didn't get a good vibe from the information I shared with her about him, which wasn't fair because she had never met him. Besides, she wasn't the best judge of character when it came to relationships. I said that because of the current relationship she'd been in for the past two years—but I digressed. This story is about me, not her.

Tamaika is very outspoken. When I call her to vent about my relationships, she says, "Winnie, I don't know why you're still messing with those losers. You need to cross over to the split and leave that dick alone."

I tell her, "No thanks, sister. I'm strictly dickley, and *you* need to get on the right track, grab this iron and hold on tight."

"You need to figure out what you want and then you'll pick the right man."

"I know what I want, but no *one* man has it all. Between the three men I have met recently, they each bring something different to the table, which adds up to the ten things I'm looking for in a man. If I could wrap them up into one person, I would have the perfect guy."

"You need to see a psychiatrist and get your head examined because there's no way you can use men as pick-a-parts to make your perfect man. They aren't automobiles, you know, although I would love to just cut men up, period."

"Bye, girl. You're talking crazy. I have to go, Sean is on his way over."

"What are you guys getting into tonight?"

"He has a friend that plays the sax in a jazz band. He's in Pasadena tonight at Red, White and Bluzz."

"What are you wearing?"

"I'm wearing a black short romper with my four-inch black peep-toe booties. We are going to look like Kimora Lee and Russell Simons tonight when I put those shoes on." We laughed.

"All right, have fun. I'll talk to you later."

Tommy

The phone rang. It was Tommy, Tom-Tom, for short.

"Hi, Tom-Tom, what's up?"

"I was calling to see if I can come over tonight. I know you normally like to come over to my place, so I don't have to go out, but I thought I would accommodate you this time and come over to your house and bring dinner."

"Mmhh, tonight isn't a good time. I have another engagement to attend."

"Well, can I go with you?"

"No, I mean I'm going with a friend to a jazz event and we don't have an extra ticket."

"Okay, maybe we can go see a movie tomorrow?"

"That sounds good. I'll call you tomorrow. Bye, Tom-Tom."

I mentioned earlier, Tommy is a dine-in-only kind of guy. He had great attributes—handsome, intelligent, nice, passionate, giving, and caring. What I didn't share with you was that Tommy was not the best-dressed person in the world. I was surprised the fashion police hadn't arrested him and thrown him in jail. He wore stripes and plaid pants, and all of his pants were above the ankle like Steve Urkel. He was always clearing his throat, humming while eating, jerking his body, and yelling out words.

The real reason I was not comfortable going out with Tommy was because he had Tourette syndrome. Tourette syndrome is a neurological disorder that causes people to make repetitive, uncontrollable movements and sounds.

Shortly after we met, Tommy invited me to his house for a home-cooked dinner. I must say I was surprised. There were red and white rose petals on the floor leading from the doorway to the dining room; candles were lit throughout the house with classical jazz music playing. He cooked cheese mashed potatoes, string beans with bacon and salmon. The food was beautifully presented. It smelled good and tasted great.

After eating dinner, he was trying to ask me, "Do you want dessert?" But it sounded like "Do you want to be dessert?"

His disorder made his words sound different and louder than what they really are. So I just ate the cake because I didn't want to be like Annie Mae (Tina Turner) from "What's Love Got to Do With It." Eat the cake, Annie Mae, eat the cake.

I remember another time when Tommy and I were watching a love story. We both got caught up in the moment, and he reached over to kiss me. I thought he was going to peck my lips off. He kissed like an ostrich. Those birds eat with a fast, rapid motion with their powerful beaks. To watch them, you would think they are going to eat through their feeding bowl.

Well, that was how it felt when Tommy was kissing me, fast, repetitive, and powerful. He was a horrible kisser, but his repeated, quick motions paid off in other areas, if you know what I mean. Depending on how you look at it, Tourette syndrome had its pros *and* cons.

Sean

The Bluzz Club was off the chain. Sean and I were enjoying each other, the nice ambience, and everyone in the club was having a good time. Sean and I had great chemistry. Whenever we went out together, people thought we were married. I couldn't deny it I was feeling him.

When we first started talking, I thought he was too quiet. I'm not a big talker, but I do expect the person I'm talking with to join in on the conversation or at least nod his head, acknowledging he is following me. He didn't say too much, and I would mostly have to guess what he was thinking.

After our first date, I saw a different side of him. He was funny, smart, and a savvy businessman who loved helping others. He was also financially stable—which was a plus—because it's one of the things on my top-10 list of finding Mr. Right, but he could use help in the fashion department. Between Sean and Tommy, I would say Sean was the better dresser, but the fashion police wouldn't pass him up either. They would write him a ticket or two.

His friend's jazz group, Night Grove, was playing awesome music—Earth, Wind & Fire, the O'Jays, Johnny Hartman, and Louis Armstrong. It had a great variety for the mixed crowd.

All the women in the club were trying to get to the front of the stage to get a good look at Sean's friend, Deshawn. He was cute but not as cute as Sean. The night was going as planned—dancing, good music, and drinks. I could not ask for a better night. After all the drinking and dancing, I excused myself to go freshen up.

As I left the restroom, I thought I heard a familiar voice. It sounded like Buck, the truck driver. When I moved closer to say hello, Sean said, "What's going on? You look like you've seen a ghost."

I played it off and said, "No, I thought I heard a familiar voice."

Throughout the night, things became strained for me and Sean. I'll bet he's thinking, "What's going on in her mind?" I am afraid he has picked up on what I am thinking.

You see Sean is very observant. He likes to watch and study people to find out what they're all about. We could be out enjoying one another and he started people watching. He could tell what, kind of people they were, what type of careers they had, if they were a couple, if they were happy or not, and how long they'd been together. And there were times when he was right. One day we took the boat over to Catalina Island, and there was a couple on board. An older gentleman with a younger woman. After watching them for hours, he said the gentleman was a doctor, that was his new wife, and they were in love. I asked Sean "How do you know that?" He replied, "Ask him," so I did. I asked the male if he was a doctor, and he said yes and went on to introduce the lady with him as his wife of six months. I was blown away. So you can see why I'm concerned he might know what I'm thinking.

As the night rolled on, we picked up where we left off—enjoying each other's company. We danced as if it was our first high school sock hop dance and never departed from one another's side.

Buck

The next day, I received a call from Buck.

"Hey, Winnie, what's up?" Buck said.

"Nothing much. Just cleaning around the house. My mom is coming over to spend the weekend with me."

"Oh okay, I made it in from Florida Thursday night. You've been on my mind, and I called to see if we could hook up tonight. It didn't help when I was at a jazz club last night, and I saw a lady that reminded me of you."

"Oh, really?" I said.

"Yes really, I was meeting my boy up there. He invited me to hear his friend who played the sax in one of the local jazz bands. They were playing at the Red, White and Bluzz Club in Pasadena. He knew how much I liked jazz, that real classic jazz, like Louis Armstrong, Frank Sinatra, Lena Horne, and Nat King Cole. So I stopped by to catch the set and say hello.

"You don't know nothing about that."

"I know all about that life. That's all my parents played around the house when I was growing up."

"Me too. Okay, I learned something new about you. I like that. Well, did you get to see your boy, the one who invited you?"

"Yeah, but he and his friend in the band were with their lady friends. I didn't want to invade their space, so I left early. They were coupled off. And you know me, I don't like being the fifth wheel."

"Did you meet his lady friend?" I asked.

"No, she was in the restroom, and he was waiting for her. But I did meet his friend Deshawn's girl. They were cool and all, but I just don't believe in being a fifth wheel."

"I understand about being the fifth wheel, I don't like feeling out of place either."

My heart dropped and my knees got weak. I was sweating as I put two and two together, and it added up to Buck and Sean being friends.

"Okay, let's get together soon."

"That sounds good. I miss you."

"I miss you, too, Buck. When are you going back on the road?"

"I'm off for the next two weeks. I have some business I need to take care of, so I'll be around for a while."

"Cool, I'll chat with you soon!"

Oh, my god, I remembered Sean looking at me as if I'd seen a ghost. I knew the voice sounded familiar, but I didn't see Buck. That wasn't cool at all! Sean and Buck knew each other! That was the last thing I needed.

I'd been out of the dating scene for a while and just when I got back in, that was what happened—I met two guys who happened to be friends. I was not a player and didn't have the time or skill to figure that thing out.

Wow, I needed my sister for that one. She'd been playing girls from the beginning, and that time I needed her help.

I was just getting to know Buck, and I liked what I had with him. I'd been dating Sean for over ten months, and I could see us with a house on the hill, all the amenities, and the toys that go along with it.

Each man brought something different to the table. I would like to spend more time getting to know Buck, but the thing may come crashing down before I get the chance. Then I'd be stuck with Tommy, Tom-Tom for short, and I was not feeling him like that. Tommy was cool to kick it with and he made me laugh, but I was not ready for someone to be yelling at me all the time.

"Hey, sis, what are you doing? I need to talk to you."

"What's up? How was your date last night with Sean?"

"It was nice. He's a true gentleman and so easy to get along with. We can talk about any and everything. His friend's jazz band was great, and the music selections were nice. The entire atmosphere put me and Sean in a comfortable, romantic place. But I called to tell you what happened. When I went to the little girls' room, I thought I heard a familiar voice that sounded like Buck's."

"Buck, the truck driver?"

"Yes."

"Well, was it him?"

"I'm not sure. When I was headed in that direction, no one was there but Sean. Sean was looking at me in a strange way, and said, 'Are you okay? You look like you've seen a ghost?' I said, 'Yes, I'm good.'

"Tamaika, I know I heard what I heard."

"Well, what happened after that?"

"Sean was quiet for some time and after a few hours, we continued to dance and enjoy each other's company again. He didn't mention anything, but I could tell he was still thinking about it. Well, the next day, I got a phone call from Buck asking to see me. When I told him my mom was coming over to spend the weekend with me, he said, 'Okay, but I've been thinking about you.' He went on to say he was at Red, White and Bluzz last night."

"Isn't that the club you and Sean went to?"

"Yes, But let me finish. He said there was a lady there that reminded him of me."

"Did he see you?"

"I don't know. I'm not sure. I was in the restroom. He goes on to say that he was meeting a friend there. But his friend was with his lady, and the band player's girlfriend was there too, so he didn't want to be the fifth wheel. Anyway, a long story, short... he didn't meet his friend's lady because she was in the restroom. Do you get it now?"

"Yes, you were the lady friend of *his* friend."

"Yes, that's it! Sean and Buck are friends. Is this ironic or what? Who would have known that these two guys would be friends? I'm starting to like Sean a lot, too."

"Well, what about Tom-Tom?"

"Girl, that's a long story. I haven't told you everything about him, that's a story and conversation we must have over lunch with a glass of wine." LOL

"What are you going to do?"

"I don't know, but I'm not committed to either one of them, and they both know I'm dating. Sean always expresses his feelings toward me, and tells me he can see us having a life together. I can see it, too, but I'm taking it slow and playing it cool. With Buck, the verdict is still out. He says a lot of crazy stuff and plays a lot, so I don't take him seriously. He has some good qualities, but I need more time with him. And Tommy, I know I will never settle down with him. He's a lot of fun, so passionate and giving."

"I hope he doesn't know Sean or Buck." We laughed at the idea.

"We're laughing now, but it will not be funny if he knows them both."

"Okay, Tamaika, I've had enough of this. I need to do some serious thinking. Thanks, girl. I'm glad you're my sister. I can always count on you when I'm going through my situations. You never judge me."

"You're my little sis. I got you! I still think you should cross over to the split side..."

"No thanks, it's not that bad yet. I'll talk to you later. Love you!"

"I love you, too."

Tommy

With everything that was going on, I needed to get away to collect my thoughts.

I'd call Tom-Tom to get away from it all. I' was sure I'd be safe there. There was no way I would run into Sean or Buck at his house. A movie day with Tommy sounded like a good way to take my mind off things. I picked up the phone and dialed his number.

"Hello."

"Hi, Tommy, Tom-Tom for short."

"Hey, Winnie, how're you doing?" "I'm good and you?

"I'm hanging... no complaints. It does no good anyway because no one wants to listen."

"You're right about that. I was calling to see what you're getting into today."

"Nothing much. Just doing something around the house."

"Can I come over? I need to be around someone I can enjoy and have fun with.

"Sure, you know I have an open door policy when it comes to you."

The whole time he was talking, he was yelling at me. Keep in mind, he has Tourette syndrome.

"That's good to know. You are so sweet. I'll be headed your way shortly."

"Okay, I'll see you soon. Bye, Winnie."

As I was on my way to Tommy's house, my phone rang. It was Sean.

"Hi, Sean."

"Hi, Winnie, how are you?"

"I'm good."

"I had a wonderful time last night."

"I enjoyed you, too. The night was beautiful, and your friend's jazz band was off the chain."

"I loved when they played 'Unforgettable' by Nat King Cole. That's how I feel about you. You are helping me trust again."

"Oh, how sweet."

"What are you getting into today?"

"I'm on my way to a friend's house to hang out. My mom is staying with me this weekend, and she can be a chatterbox. We don't see each other often so when we get together, it's like she's making up for lost time. I have a lot on my mind. and I don't want her to think I'm ignoring her or don't want her here. So I'm going to get away for a while. Plus, when I'm home I get distracted easily and start doing other things. I'm most productive when I'm away from the house. So I told her I was going to help a friend out, and I would be back by six o'clock.

"What's on your mind? Is it something I can help you with? Does it have anything to do with last night?"

"I just have a lot on my mind. Maybe I will open up to you later, but for now, I just need to figure things out.

"Okay, you know I'm good with people.

"I know. But I just need some time."

"Okay, I won't pressure you, but when you're ready to talk, I'll be here."

"Thank you. That's good to know."

"Okay, enjoy time with your friend. I'll call and check in on you later."

"You are so thoughtful."

"I know." We laughed.

"And cocky, too. Bye, Sean."

I was really feeling him, but I was so afraid if he found out I was dating his friend; that was going south real quick.

When I arrived at Tommy's place, his kids were there, and I was not feeling that that day. I should have asked him if that was his weekend with the kids. But I was there already. Hopefully, they will go in the other room and stay there.

As I was getting out my car and walking up to Tommy's house, my mind was whizzing at the thought of Sean and Buck being friends. I was not in a good place right that moment. I know I heard his voice. Plus Buck confirmed it when he called me. Anyway, I was going to block my thoughts of the other night, and Tommy's kids before I rang the doorbell, so I could enjoy Tommy and the movies.

I rang the bell. Tommy opened the door to let me in.

"Hello, Tommy—Tom-Tom, for short."

"Come on in, Winnie."

"I brought some movies. Well, my sister's friend *burned* some movies. Can you say bootleg?" (LOL) "She's going to send Hollywood into a Great Depression. I have *Twelve Years a Slave*, *American Hustle*, and *Fruitvale Station*."

"You got *Fruitvale Station*? I wanted to see that movie but missed it when it was playing on the big screen!"

"I got you, no worries. You can now watch it in the privacy of your own home. It might have people talking, laughing, and eating popcorn, but at least you will get a chance to see it. But I'm not sure if it's a movie for kids."

"The kids are in their room."

"Yeah!" I shouted with great joy.

"What?" he said, wondering why I was so excited.

"I was just mocking you. How you're always yelling out words sometimes."

He laughed and said, "Yeah, but I have a reason. You don't."

"What did you cook, or are we ordering out?"

"I have leftover pizza from last night."

"Really, I don't want that. Let's order Chinese food."

"Okay, that sounds good. Order enough for the kids, too."

"Do we have to? Just kidding."

While ordering the food, I heard voices. I'm wondering is he talking to someone. I came over for peace and quiet from my mom, and to collect my thoughts. But instead I got his kids and unwelcome friends. With my luck, it might be Sean or Buck. But I didn't want to speak that into existence. Let me erase that thought from my mind. Just when I was about to call Tommy's name, he yelled out.

"Hey, Winnie, I apologize. I wasn't trying to be rude. I was going to turn my phone off because I knew you were coming over here for peace and quiet and to spend time with me. That was one of my childhood friends. I thought he would have called before you got here. He's in town for a while and wants to get together before he heads out again. I've been waiting on his call all morning. Anyway, I'm all yours now. I'm turning my phone off."

"No worries, I just hope now I can have you all to myself."

"Yes, I'm all yours. You have my undivided attention. I will hook up with him later. Besides, I told him the woman I'm trying to make mine is over at my house."

"What do you mean, 'make yours?'"

"Winnie, you know I'm feeling you and you're feeling me, too. You just don't want to admit it."

"Whatever, Tommy, I'm not going there with you today. Can we start the movie sometime soon before the kids start moving around and then this day is going to be worse than when it started?"

"Yes, babe. Wow, that's my dawg. I'm not going to keep talking about him, but, babe, I haven't seen or talked to him in years. I can't wait to see him and introduce you."

"Who said I want to meet him?"

"Babe, you have to meet my friends. That's the only way you'll get a true idea of who I am."

"Stop calling me babe. They say the best way to find out who a person is, is to meet their family."

"Well, that goes hand and hand because my friends are my family. There are only two friends I consider family, and he is one of them. I have known him my whole life."

"Okay, if you say so."

"I told you about him before. He drives trucks."

"You never mentioned you had a friend who drives trucks. You mentioned you had a close friend that travels a lot."

"Yeah, that's him. Remember, I told you I have a friend that travels cross country, and he likes driving."

"Yeah, but I would not put two and two together that he drives trucks cross country but okay."

"I cannot wait until you meet him. I think you'll like him. He's funny. He has a saying when he gets excited about his job."

"What's that?"

"He says his name, and it rhymes with truck and fuck. Excuse my French."

"What's his name?"

"His real name is Jamal, but those of us who grew up with him call him Buck."

My eyes got big. "Buck!"

What, I just lost my appetite. I was ready to go home then. I came over there to escape from what happened the other night, and the saga continued. Oh, my lord, what am I going to do?

"Are you okay, Winnie? You're acting like I just cursed you out."

Thinking to myself, I said, "You did."

"Tommy, I just have a lot on my mind and when you mentioned your friend, it just put me in another place. I was hoping you and I could spend some time together. I could unwind, relax, and take my mind off things."

"No worries, Winnie. That's fine. Let's put our movie in. Which one you do you want to watch first?"

"It doesn't matter. We can watch *Fruitvale Station*, since you haven't seen it yet."

"Buck said he might stop by, but he's so unpredictable. You can't trust anything he says. I always tell him, 'Man, you need to make your words mean something because you play too much, and no woman will ever take you seriously.'"

That was the Buck I knew, too. I couldn't believe my life was playing out like that. I'd been out of the dating scene for over five years, and when I got back out there looking for Mr. Right, they were all linked together. I knew Pasadena was small, but I didn't think *that* small. I guess I'd better believe it.

Trying to stay focused on *Fruitvale Station* was hard. I kept waiting for the doorbell to ring and see Buck standing there. I didn't want a life with Tommy, but I didn't want to hurt him either. I was sure he was not going to be happy when he finds out I was dating his friend. I should have known they might know each other. After all, I did meet Buck when I was leaving Tommy's place. But who would have thought they were linked together?

I was not feeling that at all. I needed to call my sister.

Sean

"Sister, I need to see you. Can you come over tonight after I put Mom to bed?"

"Why then?"

"Because I have a lot to tell you, and I don't want Mom in my business. You know how Mom can get, and I don't need her two cents right now."

"Okay, I'll come over after work."

"Thanks, sis. See you tonight."

I couldn't wait to talk to Tamaika. I had so much to tell her, but I was not sure I was ready for her smart comments.

My phone rang. It was Sean.

"Hey, beautiful, how's it going?"

"It's going. My day was unbelievable, and I didn't think it could get more exciting, but it did."

"Do you care to share?"

"No, Sean, I told you I'm not ready to open up yet. I promise when I'm ready to talk, you'll be the first person I call, or at least, the second one."

"Who will be the first person?"

"My sister."

"Why her and not me?"

"Because I have known her all my life, and I know she loves me and will not hurt me. Also, she's has been in a similar situation, dealing with struggles and adversity. She's a true survivor and gives me sound advice and leadership."

"Sounds like you love and admire your sister.

"I do."

"I pray you and I can share that someday."

"Well, Sean, you never know. Someday, in the famous words of Jessie Jackson, 'Keep hope alive.'" We chuckled.

"Winnie, you know I'm here for you if you need to talk. I wish you would open up to me. I understand you more than you think. I truly like you... for you. I can see you and I having a life together. I like everything about you. You're smart, funny, beautiful, and God-fearing. You have a big heart, and you're giving. You've accomplished a lot in life and yet you're not vain.

"I love that you're humble and down to earth. Most accomplished women make it a point to let you know they have their own money. They have that 'I don't need you' attitude.' You're a woman worth waiting for and I don't have anything but time. So I'll be patient and wait. I'll be here when you're ready."

"Wow, thank you, Sean! I appreciate the kind words. It's not easy for me to open up and trust after my marriage ended behind cheating. I know I have to move on, and I have, for the most part. It's going to take time for me to fully open myself up to someone else again. I don't want to bring my past into my future, to ruin it.

"At the same time, I have to make sure I have let my past go. I don't want to bring the old hurt into my new relationship. When I'm in a relationship, I want to allow the person to make his own mistakes and not the mistakes my past brings. I just need more time. But I will let you in on a little secret."

"What's that?" he asked.

"I like you, too. More than I lead on." I smiled and I could hear him smiling, too. "Okay, handsome." That was my name for him; he calls me beautiful.

"I'll talk to you tomorrow. My sister is coming over tonight."

"You girls are going to have some *me* time?"

"Yes."

"Well, you enjoy each other and let's get together tomorrow after you take your mom home."

"Okay, talk to you later."

Tamaika was on her way over, and I could not wait to tell her what had happened. First things first, let me check to see if I have any leftovers because this girl loves to eat. She was thin as wind but could put away some food. When you see her, you see more feet than body. I was laughing at the thought, but I'd better not let her hear me say that.

The doorbell rang; it was Tamaika.

"Hey, sister."

"Don't 'Hey, sister' me. What's wrong with you that I had to come over here at night?"

"I love my sister and need to talk to you. I'm glad you came.

"You will not believe what I'm going to tell you. Remember when we were joking about Tommy knowing Sean and Buck?"

"Yeah."

"Well, guess what, he does. He and Buck are childhood friends!"

"What the what! Winnie, stop playing."

"I wish I was! He mentioned his childhood friend that travels all over, but he said his name is Jamal. While that's his birth name, his childhood friends from the neighborhood call him Buck. Then he confirmed it when he said he drives a truck and has a saying about driving the truck and fucking. I was like... that's Buck! I thought I would pass out. I lost my appetite, and you know how much I like to eat."

"Oh no, are you sure? You know how you've been hearing things lately."

"Yes, sister, I'm sure. I know what I heard."

"What are you going to do?"

"I don't know. That's why I called you to come over. My head is killing me right now, trying to figure all this out. This is the last thing I need. It's like I hit the lotto, but I have to give the prize back."

"Wow, calm down, take a deep breath, and think about everything that has happened this weekend. It's like your life is coming full circle in a short time. You need to figure out which one of these guys you really like and tell him the situation. He will understand if you tell him now while it's still early."

"It's been almost a year. That's not early."

"You have been dating these guys for almost a year, and you're just now finding out they know each other?"

"Yes."

"You never met any of their friends or family?"

"No."

"And you didn't think that was strange?"

"No, not really because I wasn't trying to do all that. I was just dating them and having fun. And Buck is out of town a lot, so I rarely spend time with him. I have met Sean's mom, dad, and some family members but very few of his friends. I'm still not sure if Sean and Buck are friends because remember when I went over to say hello, Sean was by himself, and he looked at me strangely and said I looked like I had seen a ghost. So I never got the chance to confirm it."

"Do you feel comfortable talking to Sean and asking him about his friends to see if he has one named Buck?

"I don't know, Tamaika. Not really."

"Well, Tommy will probably yell at you, but he does that anyway, so you won't know if he's angry or not." She laughed.

"That's not funny, Tamaika. He has a problem."

"What kind of problem?"

"That's right, I haven't told you, huh?"

"Told me what?"

"I wanted to have this conversation over lunch in a public setting because I know how you can be when you're trying to clown. I want to keep this conversation in perspective."

"What's wrong with him, is he retarded?"

"Tamaika, don't use that word anymore. Better to say, does he have a disability?"

"Well, does he?"

"Ugh, you are making this hard for me. Tommy has Tourette Syndrome."

"He has what?" She giggled. "Maybe you need to be with Tommy. You two are two peas in a pod. You are crazy and he can yell, grunt, and use his jerky movements to knock the crazy out of you."

LOL

"That's nothing to laugh at or make fun of, Tamaika. You can be so insensitive at times."

"I'm sorry, Winnie. It's funny that you would be attracted to someone like that."

"I didn't know until we started hanging out. He has such a big heart and is a very good person. I thought it would be cool because I only see him in-house."

"What do you mean in-house?"

"Tommy is a dine-in-only kind of guy."

"Winnie, are you crazy? I don't know how you thought you were going to pull that off. That's a grown man. Didn't you meet him in a public place?"

"Yeah, but when I found out that he likes movies, I thought to myself this is a good way to keep him inside... dinner and a movie. So that's when I started calling him my dine-in only date."

"You really are crazy, but let me make myself clear. I wasn't laughing at his condition because I had to overcome my own struggles in dealing with life issues. When I was going through the storm, I had to reach out and get help. I learned I couldn't do it by myself. I just pray he is getting the help he needs to live a normal life. Whatever living a normal life means because truth be told, we all have issues and are dealing with something. The most important thing is *how* you deal with it and overcome. With God, family, and the support of true friends, you can handle all things."

"Wow, sister, that shows growth."

"Yes, it does, and it took me to go through something tough to get to this point. You know what they say, 'No one cares about another person's problem until it affects them or hits home.' Tommy mentioned this friend from out of town before, but we never talked too much about him."

"Does he raise his kids?"

"Yes and no. He has weekend visits."

"I can't imagine that house when all of them get together." She continued to giggle.

"Tamaika, you are having way too much fun at my expense. Stop it. His daughter has Tourette syndrome, too. His son is what some would call *normal.*"

"Girl, I just told you, none of us are normal. We all have something wrong with us but are too proud to admit it. Speaking of recognizing and admitting our faults and getting the help we need, have you been taking your meds?"

"No."

"Why not?"

"I ran out and I missed my last three doctor appointments. Don't worry. I have it on my calendar to call and reschedule my appointment for one day next week. Too much is going on in my head, and I need help sorting everything out."

"Next week? It sounds like you could use them now. That's nothing to play with, Winnie. You need to take your medicine. Please take your meds. When I was going through my stuff... God, the meds, and family is what got me through. You need to take things more seriously. Didn't you say when you take the meds, it helps you with your emotions and the racing thoughts?"

"Yeah, it does."

"Then why are you not taking them? Do any of your guy friends know you're taking medication?"

"No, it's not like that. I don't need the meds to function. Plus, I'm not serious with any of them to let them in my life like that."

"Once again, you're in denial."

"Whatever, Tamaika, you don't know what you're talking about. All right, I'm done. I've had enough of you. You can leave now!"

"I'm not going anywhere. I have to eat first. I didn't drive from Colton to Pasadena just to see you and hear about your drama. I agreed to come after work for Mom's good cooking. I knew she was going to cook because if she was waiting on you, she would starve."

Ugh! I love Tamaika, but sometimes she gets on my nerves.

"Is Mom asleep?"

"Yes, you know she goes to bed early. That's why I had you come over after work because she would be asleep. I don't want Mom all in my business. She already thinks I'm crazy."

"She might be right. I apologize. You might not be crazy, but you do need professional help."

"I thought you were leaving."

"I am after I eat."

"Well bye, let yourself out. I'm going to bed."

"Okay, I'll check in on Mom and then I'm out."

Mom and Tamaika thought I need medication because of my mood swings. I didn't agree with them. I just got tired of people and needed time to myself.

There were moments when I was feeling down, depressed, and my mind was spinning out of control, but when I stepped away from it all—take a minute to myself—everything was all right. Although I had to admit that didn't always work. There were times when my thoughts seemed as though they came alive and took total control of me. At that point, I did take my medication, and it helped me control those thoughts. I'd feel better, but that didn't mean I needed to be on continuous medication. It drove them crazy when I didn't take my meds because they said I should take them every day—like my life depended on it.

While I said, it was my life and I was in charge of me.

Buck

After leaving Tommy's place, I didn't feel like talking to anyone but my sister. I had to admit, she shocked me with her response about Tommy. I just knew she was going to roast me, but I guess we all have to grow up sometime. That girl never ceased to amaze me. Life surely had a way of humbling us.

I missed three calls. It was Buck. I did tell him I would call him later. As I dialed his number, I realized that would be a good time to take my meds.

"Hey, Buck, what's up?"

"Nothing. Is your mom still at the house?"

"Yes, she's spending the weekend with me, remember?"

"I really want to see you."

"I want to see you, too. I'm taking her home tomorrow, but I have plans after that. My sister just left. Let me call her to see if she will come back and stay with Mom. If so, I'll call you and we can hang out. Are you down?"

"Yeah, I'm down. But does your mom need a babysitter?"

"No, she's a big girl, but I don't like leaving her alone at night when she's with me. Besides, this is my mom, not yours."

"I'm just saying."

"Well, you better stop saying before you talk yourself out of date."

"Okay cool, let me know what's up. Maybe we can catch a late movie."

"I'll see what's playing, check movie times and call you around eleven? I think the latest movie time is midnight."

"Cool, check and hit me back."

"What do you want to see?"

"I'm open but no chick flick."

"*The Wolf of Wall Street* started last Friday. Leonardo DiCaprio plays in that movie. I like him. He's up for an Oscar for best actor."

"Look at you, you think you know what's going on. I don't keep up with that stuff because I'm on the road a lot," said Buck.

"No worries, I'll keep you up to date. I'll check movie times for that show. By the way, do you know a guy by the name of Tommy? He calls himself Tom-Tom for short."

"Yeah, that's my boy. We've been friends since childhood. My mom and his mom are good friends. We lived next door to each other growing up.

He's like a brother to me. As a matter of fact, I spoke with him when I came into town, but he was entertaining his girl. Seems like everyone can get in touch and hang out with their girl but me."

"You are always on the go."

"Why do you ask?" Buck asked, curiously.

"I just found out a friend of mine is seeing him."

"Are you that friend?" he asked, suspiciously.

My heart skipped a beat. "Why would you say that?"

"You know, y'all women have game. You talk about yourself as a third person, knowing all along that friend is you." He laughed, but I didn't think it was funny.

"Okay, Buck, once again, you're going off the deep end. Got to go. Let me call my sister, I'll chat with you later."

"Peace out!"

Oh, my god, my heart was doing monkey flips. I could not believe what I just heard. That couldn't be happening to me.

Tommy

I left Tommy's house so fast, he didn't know what happened. He called to check up on me, to make sure I was okay and that I made it home safely.

"Hey, Winnie, are you good?"

"I'm good. I just had an epiphany after hearing about your friend."

"What happened? We were enjoying the movie then you started acting like you were hearing voices, telling you to get out of here. I don't understand. Is there something you want to tell me?"

"No, I'm not sure what happened. Something came over me, and I just reacted. Tommy, I have to ask you something, but I need to ask you in person. Can I see you later?"

"Sure, I told you I have an open-door policy when it comes to you."

"Yes, I remember. I'm going to church with my mom. Hopefully she will go to lunch with some of her church friends. They're called the Golden Girls like the TV show."

"Really, is your mom the Blanche of the group?" He chuckled.

"Funny. No, but there is one in the group." We both laughed. I smiled at the thought of my mom acting like a hot tail. She'd better not be like Blanche. Let me erase that idea.

"Anyway," I said, "I'll come over after church or when I drop my mom off."

"That's cool. We need to get to the bottom of this. Will you be honest and tell me why you ran out?"

"Yes, that is part of the reason I want to talk to you in person and not over the phone. I have several questions, and I need answers. I want us to be honest with each other, no matter how hard it may be."

"Okay, no problem. I can do," he replied.

"Should I pick up something to eat?"

"No, I cooked your favorite, salmon, green beans, and mashed potatoes. I also bought a key lime pie from Marie Callender's. I know how much it reminds you of your mom's lemon pie."

"Mmh, that sounds delicious. Are the kids there?"

"No, I took them home shortly after you left. I wanted to spend some alone time with you, and I didn't think you would be totally open with me if the kids are around."

"Thank you, Tommy. You are always so thoughtful. That's one of the reasons I like being with you. You always know what to do without me saying it."

"You're my girl, whether you accept it or not."

"I don't have time to go back and forth with you Tommy. I'll see you later."

"See you soon. Bye for now."

My mom and I arrived at church. As she greeted her friends, I looked at them, trying to figure out which one was Blanche. I prayed it wasn't my mom. I'd be okay with her being Dorothy or even Sophia but not Blanche.

I arrived at Tommy's house around six o'clock. I was sure he's looking good, but I knew when he opened his mouth, the smooth sexiness would fly out of the window, and the erratic words and gestures began.

I smile at the thought of it.

Knock, knock!

"Welcome, I hope you're hungry," Tommy said, stepping aside to let me enter.

"I can eat." Just as I imagined, Tommy was looking good in his black body shirt, black slacks, and square-toed Stacy Adams. I was surprised, because he never wore two things that matched. Just as I was going to give him a compliment, I looked down and his slacks were above his ankles. I smiled, saying to myself, "That's my Tommy." His head was perfectly shaven, and his neatly trimmed goatee accentuated his beautiful smile. The dining room looked just as gorgeous with candles burning and music playing softly in the background. The table was set with fine china, and at my seat, there was a poem he'd written for me. That was one thing I could say about Tommy, he knew how to make me feel special.

"Well, I'm impressed. This is very nice of you, making me feel like a queen."

"Anything for you. You know I think very highly of you. You are truly a blessing and a real genuine woman, which is hard to find these days."

"Well, don't forget, my hair isn't real. Other than that, you're right. I am a real woman." We laughed.

"You know what I mean. Most women just want you for what you can do for them or give them, especially when they think you have hang ups… acting like they are doing you a favor by allowing you to be in their presence. But you look past my faults and accept me for who I am."

I felt bad then. Although I enjoy being with Tommy, I knew deep down inside I couldn't have a life with him, especially after meeting Sean.

"Tommy, I do accept you, for you, as you accept me, for me. With that being said... Cheers, a toast to us and a growing friendship!"

"Speaking of friendship, I'm glad you brought that up. What happened?"

"What are you talking about?"

"Your mood changed when I brought up my friend Buck's name and mentioned he might stop by."

"That's what I wanted to talk to you about. I think I know him. He talks to a friend of mine." Oh, my god, I was doing exactly what Buck said women did—used ourselves as a third person.

As we got deeper into the conversation, I heard the doorbell ring. I asked Tommy if he was going to get the door. He excused himself, and I heard a familiar voice. Oh, my god... it was...

Buck

"Hey, you, what's up? I've been trying to reach you. I thought you were going to hit me up after you talked to your sister?"

"My sister never answered, and my mom was already asleep. I didn't want to wake her to tell her I'm leaving, as it's hard for her to fall back to sleep. Plus, I don't want to leave her alone."

"Winnie, you're not right. You stood me up. Anyway, I'm going to give you one more chance. I want you to meet one of my childhood friends. We've been friends forever. With me gone all the time, I don't get to see him that often. But whenever I'm in town, I try to hook up with him. He's excited about this new girl he's been dating for a while and wants me to meet her. He says she's the one. Because he's a special character, and normally when women find out about him, they leave, or try to use him. But this woman is still hanging around. He said she's attentive to his needs, he can talk to her about any and everything, and they have fun together. You know what they say, 'If you can make a woman laugh, and you can have the key to her heart.'"

"Oh Lord, please help me," she said to herself. "What's wrong with him?" I said, as if I don't already know.

"He has a condition with his central nervous system that causes him to twitch, jerk his shoulders, and make loud sounds while he flexes his jaws. He can stop it but not for long periods of time."

I asked, "Does he have Tourette syndrome?"

"Yes, that's what he has. I couldn't think of the term, but he doesn't let that stop him. He's a good guy though. He deserves a good woman, and he really likes this one. He wants me and my girl to hang out with them. I was looking forward to it because I haven't seen him or you in a minute. We were supposed to hang out anyway, but you stood me up. You owe me."

"Okay, Buck." I replied.

"Plus, I want to show my lady off, too. You know as I think about it, you and Tommy would make a good couple. You have your special moments and always saying you need time alone because your mind is racing with unwelcomed thoughts and voices. I must admit, you scare me when you say that because I'm not sure if you're playing or not. I just brush it off and say to myself, 'She's too fine to be crazy.' And if so, I just have to deal with it... adding her to the list of special people in my life. I guess we all have voices in our head that we debate with from time to time." Then he snickered.

"Forget you, Buck." We both laughed. "Well, I'm not ready to meet your friends, but we can still hang out one-on-one."

"That's fine. I just want to spend more time with you. We have great conversations, and I like being with you. But at some point, you will have to meet my peeps and my boys. We're all very close, and I want you to meet them."

"Where does your other friend live?"

"He stays in the Inland Empire area."

"What's your friend's name that lives in the IE?"

Buck paused. "You don't know him. Why do you ask? You said you didn't want to meet my friends."

I shrugged. "Just curious."

"My boys and I are planning a Baja Mexico cruise. I would like you to go with me."

"Oh, that sounds like fun. Who's going?"

"Me, Tommy, and one of our other homeboys. I'll keep you posted. Don't flake out on me, because you are known for that when it comes to going out with me."

"I won't. I like cruises." I said to myself, "Lord, how am I going to do this? I'm sure Tommy will also ask me to be his date? Here I go again putting myself in awkward situations." "Okay, keep me posted on the dates so I can make arrangements."

"Cool."

He changed the subject without confirming going out with his friend. I was hoping he forgot about going to the movies with them. Just when I thought the coast was clear, he said, "About hooking up with my friend and his girl, are you down?"

"I have something else planned tonight. Let me know when and I'll see what I can do."

He replied, "Here we go again. Okay, Winnie, did I scare you when you went out on the road with me?"

"What are you talking about?"

"Ever since you went out on the road with me, you act as if you're too busy or never have time."

"No, I'm good. I really enjoyed myself."

He sighed and said, "From the way you're playing dodge ball, I can't tell."

"Cute, Buck. But I'm not playing dodge ball."

He chuckled. "Okay, keep me posted. I hope you can go. You'll enjoy yourself, I promise."

"If you put it like that, I'm in."

"Okay, we'll chat soon."

Sean

I really had to get myself together with all those men. I like Sean, but he was a workaholic. His job kept him busy and on the go. Tommy was a very good companion and liked having fun, and Buck could show me the world if I open up and give him a chance. Who would have known when I started dating again, I would meet three men who were friends, and I would take an interest in *all* of them. People said there was a shortage of men once you reach a certain age, but I was in my forties. I had a lot of problems, but finding a man wasn't one of them. I was going crazy trying to figure the situation out.

Sean was a hopeless romantic, pleasing in the bedroom and a hard worker. He was every woman's dream. If I had to put the men in order of my interest, Sean would be first, Tommy second, and Buck third.

Tommy had his issues, but he was really a good man. He listened to me and didn't try to fix my problems. He allowed me to vent, and at the end of the day, that was all I need. I just wanted to vent, get those issues off my chest, and let it go. He understood me, and he was a good cook, too. That was a huge plus, considering I didn't like to cook.

Buck was cool. We had nice conversations and all—he had a good job, but there was something about him that I just couldn't quite put my finger on. We needed to spend more time together so I could figure it out. Between Buck, Sean, and Tommy, I didn't have a lot of time. Buck was on the road a lot, and when he came to town, our schedules conflict.

Oh, my god, I went with Buck once on a short run from Ontario (California) to Phoenix (Arizona). He was just telling me how nice it was for us to spend time together, and I was a breath of fresh air. He loved driving, seeing different parts of the country and wanted us to share this experience of a lifetime together. I thought that was cool then he started that mess he always said when he talked about driving, "My name is Buck, I drive a truck, and I like to fuck." He licked his lips, looking over at me.

I was getting scared because he started telling me how he could pull over, and we could make out in the corner of his truck. I looked in the back, behind the driver's seat, thinking to myself, *"There's a twin-sized bed back there. Why can't we use it?"* I didn't sound too scared, huh? LOL. Then he started ranting about lot lizards. I asked him what were lot lizards.

For those of you who are like me, not familiar with trucker's terminology—lot lizards are hookers. They're at every truck stop, walking around, looking for men to pick up, and offering sexual favors for money. I was shocked. I had to ask, "Have you ever picked up a lot lizard?" He said no, but the way he responded and kept going on about it made me wonder.

But I digress. Let's get back to Sean. He would be my ideal guy. Although there were times when we were together, I felt weird, as if he was studying me, trying to get inside my head to figure out what was going on. He told me, "I know you better than you think I do."

For instance, Sean told me I reacted oddly to unfamiliar noises. He said it happens often, but he just let it go—allowing me to be me. I was not sure what he meant by that, but because he was so handsome, I let him get away with it for the moment. Then it was those times when I believe he was not feeling me. Although he professed how much he cared about me, I still questioned it.

I could recall two occasions when I thought Sean didn't want to be involved with me anymore: Once, we went to the jazz club to see his friend perform, and another time, we were celebrating his promotion at Ruth's Chris restaurant. The conversation was flowing nicely, and out of nowhere, my personality changed. He said I was reacting strangely, started to panic, and said I wanted to leave because a friend of mine was headed toward our table. He was so considerate about the situation and suggested we leave if I didn't feel comfortable. He grabbed our things, and we left. He never mentioned anything else about that night.

After that incident, it took him a while to call me. I was concerned because I didn't know what he was thinking. Did he think I was crazy, that I had too much baggage, and he didn't sign up for that? My mind was racing. Three days later, he called and asked me out again. I was back in the game.

Tommy

Oh, my god, I heard his voice, and I panicked.

"Tommy, are you going to get the door?"

"Yes, babe."

I headed to the bathroom. My heart was beating 50 miles per hour, hoping it was not who I thought it was, but I knew that voice anywhere.

"Hey, man, what's up? I was in the neighborhood and decided to drop by. I hope that's cool. If not, too bad." They laughed and continued speaking their male jargon.

"What's up, man? It looks like you have company."

"Yeah, my girl is here. We were talking about Jamal."

"What's that fool up to?"

"Being himself... talking about his road trips, all the different states he travels through and those lot lizards. He's still messing with those lot lizards." They chuckled.

"That's Jamal. You know that boy will never change. It's going to take a special woman to change him. Speaking of special ladies, where is your girl... this famous lady you've been telling me about?"

"She's in the restroom. Babe, are you all right? I want to introduce you to my friend."

My heart was still beating fast. Tommy was walking down the hall toward the bathroom. All I could hear was the floor cracking and the voices in my head. My heart was pounding and my mind was spinning out of control, telling me to run, act like I was taking a shower. Do this, do that, all kinds of crazy stuff. At that moment, I wished I could turn off those voices and thoughts. I didn't know *who* to listen to or what to do at that point. What can I do to get out of this mess?

I walked to the bathroom door, tripped on the carpet, and hit my head on the toilet. While losing consciousness, I could hear male voices asking me if I was all right.

When I came to, I was in the hospital with blurred vision and memory loss, going in and out of consciousness. I could hear people talking but not able to make out what was being said. There was one voice that stood out. It was my sister. I wondered, "What is she doing here?" Then I passed out.

"Hello, my name is Sean, Dr. Sean Jackson. I'm the ER physician, and I'll be monitoring your sister."

"What happened? What's wrong with her?"

"Your sister has a concussion. She fell, hit her head, and she's suffering from memory loss."

"How serious is it?"

"It's common after most head injuries and could be very serious if she has internal bleeding from the brain. Thank God, she didn't crush her skull. We will run more tests to make sure she's not bleeding internally. If there's no bleeding in the brain, we don't have to perform surgery. The recovery process should not be too painful. But it will be a long recovery, and she will need family support. With that being said, once she gets her memory back, she should recover 100 percent and return to performing her normal day-to-day activities. She may need rehab, so I want you to be prepared if that's an option, but let us do our job, and I'll keep you posted."

"Praise God. That's good news. I thought I had lost my sister. Any idea how long it will take her to recover if she doesn't need surgery?"

"About three to four months if she responds to all the treatments and medications without a negative reaction."

"When can I see her?"

"Shortly."

"Okay, I'm going to call my mom. I didn't want to alert her until I had more information. My mom worries about her a lot. She always says, she wants Winnie to find a nice man to grow old with, so she won't be all alone."

"Your mom sounds like a wonderful woman, one who loves and cares about her daughters. Your sister is a lot like your mom... caring and gracious."

"What did you say? How do you know my sister is caring and gracious?"

"I know your sister very well."

"How well?"

"Your sister and I have been going out for a while now. I'm her friend, Sean. She never mentioned me? I was talking to her on the phone one day while you both were at your mom's house."

"Wow, you're Sean, huh? Well, to be honest, she mentioned other guys, too, so I apologize for not recognizing the name."

"No need to apologize."

"There is one guy she talked about in particular that I do remember. She said he yells at her, but it turns out, he has Tourette syndrome. I believe his name is Tommy. She was headed over to his house the last time I spoke with her."

"There are no other guys."

"What are you talking about?" Tamaika said. "Sounds like you have a lot to say, and it's not about getting my sister well."

Sean said, "I'm going to take good care of your sister, but I need you to know there are no other guys. I'm Tommy."

"What the what? Hold on, I have to call my mom. I'll be back to talk to you. I have a lot of questions."

"Oh, my god," said Tamaika. She couldn't believe her sister was in the hospital, and she was hearing those words from the good ol' doctor. She was so confused, shaking her head as she called Mom.

"Hello, Mom."

"Yeah."

"Were you asleep?"

"No, child, what's going on?"

"I'm here at the Kaiser hospital. Winnie had an accident!"

"Is she okay? What happened?"

"She hit her head. She has a concussion. But the doctor says if she doesn't need surgery, she should be fine. He said she didn't crush her skull, which is good news, but they are going to run more tests to make sure she's not bleeding internally or in the brain."

"Oh, my god, Lord, watch over my baby and those doctors who're looking after her. Okay, I'm getting dressed, and I'm on my way!"

"Okay, Mom, one last thing, I need to prepare you for..."

"What, what's going on?"

"Remember the guy, Sean, she said she's dating?"

"Yes, what about him?"

"He's a doctor, her doctor... but there's a lot more to this story, Mom."

"What the what! Shut the front door! I'm on my way."

"Drive safely, Mom."

"Okay, daughter, see you soon."

Tamaika hung up the phone, walked back over to Sean (Dr. Jackson) while she's bewildered, and thought she didn't believe that. The girl had always something brewing in the pot with or without her being there.

"So, Dr. Sean Jackson, we have to talk. How well do you know my sister?" Tamaika said.

"Very well, I've been dating Winnie for several months and have found out some interesting things about her. Did you know your sister was diagnosed with a mental illness disorder called schizophrenia?"

"No, what does that mean?"

"Good question." Dr. Sean Jackson explained, "Schizophrenia is a brain disorder that distorts the way a person thinks, acts, expresses emotions, perceives reality, and relates to others."

Tamaika asked, "So hitting her head didn't fix the problem?"

He smiled. "No, it's more complex than that. If it was that easy, I would be out of a job. There would be no need to pay me the big bucks to diagnose and treat the problem. It would be easy for me or any other doctor to suggest to the patient suffering with schizophrenia or any other mental illness disorder to go hit their head on something and snap out of it." They both chuckled, weakly/tensely.

Tamaika was bewildered. Wow, she didn't know her sister was dealing with that. "You're right," Tamika said, "she does have a strong personality. Please don't mention this to my mom. Let me tell her later when we're at home." Tamaika was worried about her mom and didn't think she could handle all of that right then. "She may have a nervous breakdown."

"Okay, that's fine. You can tell her at your leisure," said Dr. Jackson.

Tamaika asked Sean, "Are you the one she met at the old folk's club?"

Sean replied, "Yes, that's me. We did meet at the Elks Lodge in LA. She was with your godmother, and I was there with my dad and uncle. It's an interesting story. Did she tell you she sent your godmother into the club to get me?"

"Yes, she did. And we were raised better than that. My mom always taught us to let the man make the first move."

He giggled and said, "Winnie is a beautiful woman, and I'm really shy when it comes to approaching women especially beautiful women. I didn't want to get shot down in front of my dad and uncle. So I'm glad it happened the way it did or I would have missed out on a good woman. But anyway, I figured out something was wrong when we were at the Cheesecake Factory.

"I went to the restroom. When I came back, she said, 'You are a handsome guy' as if she had never seen me before and was meeting me for the first time. I said thank you. I thought it was cute and smiled, thinking, 'Oh, yeah, she likes to role play. This will be fun.'

"As I sat down, she asked my name and if we could exchange numbers so we could chat later since she was there with a friend. That was puzzling, but I went along with it and introduced myself as Tommy... my friends call me Tom-Tom for short.

"After that exchange, I noticed a change in her attitude, and she had a blank look in her eyes. Being in the medical field, I knew something wasn't right, but I thought she was a beautiful woman, and I'll take a chance and see where this friendship goes. Clearly, there was something wrong, but we continued to see one another."

Tamaika asked, "Sean, you didn't think once about running as far as possible?"

"No, you see I'm the type of guy that doesn't need to sleep with every woman I see or have a relationship with every woman I meet.

Being a doctor, my first thought was maybe I'll continue to hang out with her, learn more about her, so I can get her the help she needs.

"After all, we're all looking for that perfect person, the one that doesn't exist. We all have flaws, but as time went on, I learned more about her and fell in love with her."

"You don't have Tourette syndrome?"

"Huh, what are you talking about?"

"Winnie said Tommy has TS, and he was always yelling at her."

Sean smiled and said, "Again that was me giving her what she needed to feel comfortable. Your sister is a God-fearing, smart, funny, adventurous, motivating, and encouraging woman. That's hard and rare to find, especially for a guy like me. Being a doctor keeps the heat on, but it doesn't bring quality women to the table. When women find out I'm a doctor, their eyes light up, and all they see is dollar signs.

"There's an old Zambian proverb that says, 'When you run alone, you run fast, but when you run together, you run far.' Your sister didn't care if I was a doctor—it didn't matter to her. She liked me, for me, and I thought I could help her through her situation, stabilize her emotions. And at the end of the day, if she still thought I was a cute, bald head guy with a gorgeous smile, then it's all good."

Tamaika thought, "That's some kind of love."

"With Winnie's mental illness disorder, she can still function and do her normal activities as long as she takes her medication."

"My mom and I told Winnie she acts differently when she's off her meds, but she kept telling us we were crazy, and nothing was wrong with her. She would tell us they were victims, and she only needed to take her meds when she's feeling down to get her energy back.

"While part of that is true, the medication does help to control Winnie's moods and keep her from going into a depression. Schizophrenia is also marked by feelings of sadness, worthlessness, or hopelessness, which is also known as bipolar. When she takes her medication, it helps to prevent those mood swings. Taking medication on a regular basis, she'll have more control over her emotions. That's why it's important for her or anyone suffering with this disorder to be consistent and continue to take their medication."

"How long has she been suffering with schizophrenia?" Sean asked.

"It happened about two years ago. I received a call from her one evening asking me to pick her up from the hospital. When I asked her what happened and why didn't she call me or Mom to be with her, she just said she wasn't feeling well and called 911. Winnie didn't want to worry us. I told her it was too late, we were already worried and please don't do that again.

"We did notice a difference in her behavior after the incident, but we had no idea it was to this magnitude. We didn't know she was diagnosed as having schizophrenia.

"Now, it's coming back to me. Oh, wow!" Tamaika said. "I remember shortly after Winnie was released from the hospital, she said she was hearing voices and felt like the voices were controlling her thoughts. I thought to myself, 'She's on that *good, good*. I need the medication she's on.'" They chuckled.

Tamaika said, "I did really think that but told her not to worry. We all have friendly voices that take over us, from time to time. She calmed down and was comfortable after that."

"Well, that's a good way to put it," Sean said, "but it's more complicated than that. Have you ever been in a dilemma or situation where you needed to make a decision and you hear voices of reasoning telling you to do something when you know it's wrong? If you have to second-guess yourself, those are the voices in your subconscious mind. Imagine being stuck in a dream, and you cannot wake up. Well, that's what your sister's situation feels like. She's awake, dealing with the dream, *and* it's her reality. It's overwhelming and the mind's thoughts move rapidly and tangentially from one idea to the next, causing her to hear voices."

"Wow, Sean, this is deep."

Sean replied, "It is. Mental illnesses are diseases that can cause mild to severe disturbances in thinking, feeling and behavior. These disturbances may significantly impair a person's ability to function, but it's a disorder that can be treated. A person can learn to cope, improve or experience a full recovery with the correct medication and resources. Once you have the knowledge and education related to disorders, you have a better understanding. You're able to help the person in their time of need."

Sean continued, "I love my job. Winnie says I'm a workaholic, but she appreciates my passion for helping others."

"So answer this question," said Tamaika, "when Winnie said she was going over Tommy's house, she was actually going over your house?"

"That's right," said Sean.

"Okay, I know all of this sounds crazy, but she couldn't tell his house looked the same as yours?"

"Tamaika, you are off the chain. She always said she didn't like everything that comes out your month, but you keep it real, and you love her unconditionally."

He laughed then explained, "Your sister never came to my house. I always picked her up and we'd go out. It so happens every time she was going through her mood swings, she wanted to talk with Tommy... Tom-Tom for short. I'm not sure why, but I think she believed she could relate to him more."

"This sh——— is complicated. Was Winnie with you when the accident happened? Let me rephrase that... Which one of you was she with when the accident happened?"

"Winnie thought she was at Tommy's house. I cooked her favorite food, and we were preparing for our night when she began fantasizing and became delusional... hearing voices of me and Tommy. I believe she thought I was going to find out about Tommy, and it was overwhelming for her.

"So she rushed to the bathroom to get away when she slipped and hit her head. I called 911, and that's how we made it to the hospital. Winnie didn't talk much about her family, but she did mention you in conversation a few times. I remembered your name and found your number in her phone."

"Quick thinking, Fifty Shades of Grey. I'm just kidding, Sean. For real though... much gratitude to you for contacting me. This is all too much for me to handle right now. I do have another question for you. I think I know the answer, but I'll ask anyway. Are you Buck, too?"

He smiled. "Yes, I'm Buck, too. At the same time, Buck is also a real person. You see, he's my childhood friend who drives a diesel truck cross country. He's a funny character and gets so excited about his job. Whenever he's talking about his work, he says, 'My name is Buck, I drive a truck, and I love to fuck.'" They both said it together and laughed, lightening the mood a bit.

"What do you know about that?" Sean asked.

"My sister told me about the men she's dating and their personalities. She was devastated when she discovered you all were friends," Tamaika said. "Now, I understand why. When she was telling me the story, I was thinking to myself, 'That's weird. Winnie has such bad luck.' How could it be that my sister would be the one woman in the world to meet three different men that all happen to be friends? She panicked, worried that you would find out about each other, and she would lose you all. Of the three of you, you're her ideal man."

"Really? I guess with everything going on, I didn't see that. But I'm willing to do whatever it takes to keep her."

"Now, you say Buck is a real person?"

"Yes, he's a real person," said Sean. "I got the idea of acting like Buck because one day, we were leaving the house, and there was a big rig parked across the street. She was ranting on about how interesting it would be to take a cross-country road trip. As always, trying to meet her every need, I told her all things are possible, and I'd love to take her on a trip.

"After listening to Buck talk about his experiences, with such excitement, I started acting like him, and she loved it. I rented a truck, and we did a short road trip to Phoenix. I will admit I found that to be a little weird, having to act everything out, even the lot lizard conversations. And I didn't feel comfortable talking with her about other women."

"What are lot lizards?"

"Hookers that walk the truck stops, looking for men to trade sex for money."

"Really?"

"Yes, really."

"Your friend Buck is out of control."

"I know. He's a special person. But that's my boy. He's got my back. If I need him, he'll be there. No questions asked."

"Wow, Sean, I can't believe what I'm hearing. I've known this girl all my life and didn't know she was suffering with mental illness. I should have noticed the changes," Tamaika admitted with sadness.

"Well, duty calls," Sean said, looking down at his watch. "I have to check on Winnie now and make my rounds. It was nice talking to you, and I look forward to meeting your mom."

"Oh, yeah, my mom. Is she here yet? I got caught up in your story about Winnie I forgot my mom was on her way up here."

"Thank you, Sean. For everything... the information you shared with me on mental illness and for taking care of my sister."

"You're welcome! I love that girl. We'll be in touch, okay?"

"Hey, Sean?"

"Yeah?"

"How can I get in touch with your friend Buck?"

"Oh, you like that craziness, huh?"

"No, I like the split, not the stick." They laughed.

"Then why do you want to get in touch with him?"

"I want the truck hook up. Maybe I can meet some lot lizards."

He laughed and walked away.

"Wow, I can't believe all this is happening. My little sister needed me, and I wasn't there for her. How could I not see what was going on? Oh man, I guess I can't beat myself up about it now. It's true what they say, 'When you know better, you do better.'

"I'm going to educate myself on mental illness disorders so I can help my sister and my mom deal with this. I smile to myself—now Winnie has a new theme song. It used to be 'This Girl is on Fire' by Alicia Keys. Now it's 'Monster' by Eminem and Rihanna. Ha, ha, ha."

I'm friends with a monster that's under my bed.

Get along with the voices inside of my head.

You trying to save me, stop holding your breath.

Now, you think I'm crazy, but that's nothing. (Eminem featuring Rihanna, "Monster")

The End

Know the Warning Signs

If several of the following is occurring, you may want to follow up with a mental health professional:

- withdrawal and loss of interested in others

- problems with concentration, memory or logical thought and speech that are hard to explain

- loss of initiation or interest in participating in activities

- An unusual drop in functioning at school, work, or social activities

- fear of going around other

- mood changes—rapid or dramatic change in feelings

If you or a loved one are experiencing any of the above symptoms, you can take action, such as

- seek help from a mental health or another health care professional

- seek counseling, support groups (one on one or group counseling)

- talk to someone you can trust and feel comfortable with

Each person's situation may vary. That's why it's important to seek professional health to get the correct help needed.

Did you know

- lime green is the ribbon color for Mental Health Awareness

- May is Mental Health Month

- mental illness is more common than heart and lung diseases combined.

- mental health disorders include but not limited to: mood swings, suicide, schizophrenia, anxiety disorders, panic disorders, obsessive-compulsive disorder (OCD), post-traumatic stress disorder (PTSD), generalized anxiety disorder (GAD), social phobia, eating disorder and more

Take the pledge to help educate and bring understanding to yourself and others throughout the year.

To learn more about mental health, please call the Fonzell Behavioral Health Resource Center at (909) 254-1147 or visit the website www.fonzellcenter.org.

NOTES

_____

_____

_____

_____

_____

_____

_____

_____

_____

_____

_____

_____

_____

_____

_____

_____

www.ingramcontent.com/pod-product-compliance
Lightning Source LLC
Chambersburg PA
CBHW050423290526
45786CB00003B/1385